Father's Promise

A Study on the Holy Spirit

F. Dean Hackett, Ph.D.

SPIRIT LIFE MINISTRIES INTERNATIONAL

Spirit Life Ministries International

Father's Promise – A Study on the Holy Spirit
Copyright © 2017 by F. Dean Hackett, Ph.D.

Formerly published © 2003
under the title *The Person and Work of the Holy Spirit*

Requests for information should be addressed to Spirit Life Ministries Publications, Hermiston, Oregon 97838

ISBN: 978-1981633128

All rights reserved. No portion of this publication may be reproduced in a retrieval system, or transmitted in any form or by any means – electronic, mechanical, photocopy, recording, or otherwise – without the express prior permission of Spirit Life Ministries Publications, with the exception of brief excerpts in magazine articles and/or other reviews.

Cover design: Aaron Hackett
Interior Design: Rosilind Jukić
Printed in the United States of America

Other books and studies by F. Dean Hackett

The Freedom Series

Agape

Discovering True Identity

Charis

The Discipleship Series

Discovering Jesus

The Joy of Becoming Like Jesus

Becoming Ambassadors for Christ

Video-based Studies available online at fdeanhackett.com

Where Are We on God's Timeclock

No Mo' Drama

21st Century Leadership 101 – Biblical Basis of Leadership Authority

With great love and appreciation this work is dedicated to my son-in-law, Mario Dučić. He is a faithful servant who is carrying the gospel of our Lord Jesus Christ to Croatia and Bosnia Herzegovina.

I love you Mario!

Table of Contents

Preface vi

Introduction x

The Promise of the Holy Spirit? 1

Who Is the Holy Spirit? 4

What is the work of the Holy Spirit? 8

How Does a Person Receive the Holy Spirit into Their Life? 12

What is the evidence of the Baptism of the Holy Spirit? 20

The Work of the Holy Spirit in Sanctification 24

The Fruit of the Spirit - a More Perfect Way 30

The Fruit of the Spirit in the Life of the Believer 36

Manifestation Gifts 44

The Importance of Holy Spirit in Your Life 54

Three Key Principles for Walking In The Holy Spirit 60

Selected Bibliography 70

Preface

We are more than a decade into the new millennium and the church in the United States and Western Europe has sunk lower into a Laodicean spirit than at any time known to modern man.

Those church movements once known for their great power and moving of the Holy Spirit are mere shadows of what they once possessed. The great "Christian Centers" of the Charismatic Renewal are museums of that great movement. Denominations who once proudly declared their faith and commitment to the Holy Spirit rarely, if ever, teach on the baptism of the Holy Spirit and the wonderful gift of speaking in tongues. Some have sunk so low they are questioning the very doctrine of speaking in other tongues as the initial evidence of the baptism of the Holy Spirit.

Jesus' command to His church has not changed.

"Behold, I send the Promise of My Father upon you; but tarry in the city of Jerusalem until you are endued with power from on high" (Luke 24:49 NKJV).

"And being assembled together with them, He commanded them not to depart from Jerusalem, but to wait for the Promise of the Father, "which," He said, "you have heard from Me; for John truly baptized with water, but you shall be baptized with the Holy Spirit not many days from now" (Acts 1:4-6 NKJV). [emphasis mine]

Where is the promise of the Father in the western church? This generation of young adults, students and children are not acquainted with the moving of the Holy Spirit and the power Jesus promised.

It must be introduced again. The church must be taught and then she must wait on Father until the Holy Spirit baptism comes in fire and power. We cannot expect to see New Testament results without New Testament power. The church will never do the works Jesus did and "even greater than these" without the baptism of the Holy Spirit.

It is for this reason I have published this series of teachings on the Holy Spirit. It is my earnest prayer we will see and experience Joel 2:28-29 in a power new way for a new generation of the church.

God bless and empower you as you study and teach these lessons on the precious person of the Holy Spirit. I give you solemn warning: These lessons are experiential. It does no good to study them and know them intellectually. You must study them and then earnestly seek to experience them and live them in your life. We are to experience the Holy Spirit and power daily!

This volume is intended to be a teacher's manual. The outlines are designed to give order and structure for the teacher to guide students through the wonderful discovery of the Holy Spirit as a person and His work in their life personally.

The outlines are not meant to be an exhaustive study in their particular subject matter. Rather, they are guidelines for personal study and structure for preparation and presentation of the material in the classroom or Bible study setting.

My prayer for you in your personal study and for the students you may be teaching is the same as the Apostle Paul's prayer for the church at Ephesus.

"Therefore I also, after I heard of your faith in the Lord Jesus and your love for all the saints, do not cease to give thanks for you, making mention of you in my prayers: that the God of our Lord Jesus Christ, the Father of glory, may give to you the spirit of wisdom and revelation in the knowledge of Him, the eyes of your understanding being enlightened; that you may know what is the hope of His calling, what are the riches of the glory of His inheritance in the saints, and what is the exceeding greatness of His power toward us who believe, according to the working of His mighty power which He worked in Christ when He raised Him from the dead and seated Him at His right hand in the heavenly places, far above all principality and power and might and dominion, and every name that is named, not only in this age but also in that which is to come. And He put all things under His feet, and gave Him to be head over all things to the church. which is His body, the fullness of Him who fills all in all" (Ephesians 1:15-23 NKJV).

Forrest Dean Hackett, Jr
November 2017

Introduction

"I not only want you to know my power and my anointing, I want to fellowship with you." The words came powerfully to my spirit, as I was worshipping the Lord.

I had been meditating on the work of Holy Spirit for several months, as part of my personal response to the one-hundred-year anniversary of the Azusa Street Revival. A deeper hunger for Holy Spirit was growing within me, as I sought the Lord through fasting and prayer. The call from Holy Spirit for "fellowship" was new and brought great anticipation. I began to search out the question, "What does it mean to 'fellowship' with Holy Spirit?"

I understood the concept and the importance of fellowship within the life-flow of a congregation. Fellowship was a significant part of the body-life in the New Testament Church. (Acts 2:42 KJV). The Apostle John encouraged fellowship with the Father and with the Son (1 John 1:1-7). Intimate fellowship with Lord, through personal worship and communion, has been a vital part of my spiritual walk for many years. How do these same concepts apply to Holy Spirit?

The Apostle Paul encouraged "fellowship of the Spirit" in his epistle to the Philippians (Philippians. 2:1-2). Fellowship is the Greek word, *koinonia*, meaning association, joint participation or communion. It carries the concept of intimacy and partnership. How does this relate to Holy Spirit and His work in a person's life?

Jesus promised Holy Spirit would come to live in the life of a believer. "And I will pray the Father and He shall give you another comforter that He may abide with you forever" (John 14:16 KJV). "Comforter" is the Greek word, *parakletos*, one who comes along beside another and is an advocate for that person. Jesus continued, *"He dwelleth with you and shall be in you"* (John 14:17). Clearly, Jesus was referring to a relationship with Holy Spirit that is to be more than casual or merely administrative.

The Apostle Paul taught the Galatians, *"If we live in the Spirit let us also walk in the Spirit"* (Galatians 5:25). The Apostle was urging, "If the Holy Spirit has made you alive, then daily live in relationship with Him." Holy Spirit is a person who longs for a deep personal relationship with each believer. Fellowship with Holy Spirit is more than Him imparting gifts or sharing His power and anointing with us. It is discovering how to "walk" with Him intimately each day and learning to clearly hear his voice.

"But it is written," wrote the Apostle Paul, *"Eye hath not seen, nor ear heard, neither have entered into the heart of man, the things which God hath prepared for them that love Him."* God has more for each person than they could ever imagine.

The Apostle continued, *"But God hath revealed them unto us by His Spirit, for the Spirit searcheth all things, yea, the deep things of God"* (1 Corinthians 2:9-10). Holy Spirit wants to reveal the "deep things" which God has prepared for each person within whom He dwells. This kind of personal conversation only happens between those who are very close and intimate.

Fellowship with Holy Spirit involves learning His personality and identifying those things that "grieve" Him (Ephesians 4:30) or may "quench" and even "reject" His influence (1 Thessalonians 4:8; 5:19). This requires a deepening personal surrender to His will that will allow Him to motivate, guide and discipline our behavior patterns and cultivate the "fruit of the Spirit."

By its very nature, fellowship with Holy Spirit requires "waiting" on Him. That is, spending large blocks of time in His presence giving Him undivided attention. Intimacy is lost when we hurry in the presence of someone. Many believers are trying to have a relationship with Holy Spirit in the same manner as a couple courting long distance or married to a workaholic. They know *about* the person but are not intimately acquainted.

The same happens when we hurry through our devotions and personal worship, not allowing for long periods of time to linger in the presence of Holy Spirit. We will only know *about* Him and not be intimately acquainted with Him and His ways. We will not learn those things that please or displease Him. Nor will we discover the secrets of God (Psalms 25:14).

Waiting on Holy Spirit, spending much time getting to know Him and becoming like Him, is a vital part of fellowship with Holy Spirit. It requires bringing our full attention upon Him in adoration that expresses passionate love and affection (Luke 24:53). Waiting requires yielding our whole being to His presence and allowing Him to drawer close and intimate. It involves receiving the expression of His love, acceptance, and affirmation to our heart. It may also require adjusting our attitude, motives and behavior so we do not grieve or quench His presence and influence in our life.

Great glory is in store for all who find "the secret place of the Most High" (Psalm 91:1). Fellowship with Holy Spirit is significant and life transforming. It is the great longing of God that each believer lives in the dynamic and the joy of this intimate relationship with the One who is "the promise of the Father."

The same assurance is true for the church family or congregation of worshippers who chose to reject the current *modus operandi* that encapsulates the worship celebration in a time structure that provides very little opportunity for waiting on the Lord.

When pastoral leadership encourages passionate desire for an intimate relationship with Holy Spirit and time is given for personal worship and adoration; the manifest presence of Holy Spirit will be restored to the worship celebration and the glory of God will be released upon His church.

Let's dig deep together. What is *Father's Promise* how can you personally receive it in your life?

The Promise of the Holy Spirit?

Objective:

Help the people discover the person of the Holy Spirit; the promise of His coming and the fulfillment of the promise.

Introduction:

The apostle Paul declared to the church at Corinth "I do not want you to be ignorant about spiritual gifts." Most English translations will have spiritual gifts in italics because the Greek text does not specifically have the word "gifts" in it. The Greek text only has the word *pneumatikoon* meaning, "spirituals." Paul is saying to the church at Corinth, "I do not want us ignorant about 'spirituals.'" Paul did not want the believers ignorant about the things of the Spirit; that is the working of the Holy Spirit. The word "ignorant" means:

- To not know
- To not understand
- To be wrong

The Apostle does not want believers to have wrong concepts and misunderstandings of the Holy Spirit and His work. It is very important that you do not lack the proper understanding or knowledge of the Holy Spirit and His work in your life and in the church. We will begin by looking at God's promise of Holy Spirit fullness.

1. What were the promises of Holy Spirit coming to mankind?

    a. The prophet Joel - Joel 2:28

    b. John the Baptist - Matthew 3:11

    c. Jesus - Luke 24:44-52; John 14:15-17

    d. The promise fulfilled - Acts 2:1-39
This is the time of the Holy Spirit. Since the day of Pentecost and the outpouring of the Holy Spirit on the 120 in Jerusalem, it is the day of the Holy Spirit.

    e. The promise is to every generation - Acts 2:38

2. The apostolic church experienced the fulfillment of the promise and encouraged all believers to seek him.

    a. When Philip went to the community of Samaria and the people turned to the Lord Jesus Christ, the Apostles Peter and John came from Jerusalem for one purpose: to pray for them to receive the Holy Spirit for they had not yet been baptized in the Holy Spirit - only in water. This is very important to understand. Many in the body of Christ teach the Holy Spirit baptism is received at salvation. In reality, the Holy Spirit takes up residence within the person at salvation. That is not the same as being baptized into the Holy Spirit. They are two distinct experiences, as exemplified here in Acts 8:14-17. The people in Samaria were saved and baptized in water. But, they were not baptized in the Holy Spirit. That happened when Peter and John lay hands on them.

b. Peter went to the home of Cornelius to preach the gospel for the first time to a Gentile audience. While he was preaching, the Holy Spirit fell upon the audience and they began to speak with other tongues. This was the first time in history for the Gentiles to receive salvation by grace and to receive the baptism of the Holy Spirit. (Acts 10:1-44)

c. When Paul met the disciples at Ephesus his first question was, *"Have you received the Holy Spirit since you believed?"* their answer was enlightening, "We have not heard there is a Holy Spirit." (Acts 19:1-7)

Closing:

God wants you to have full and correct knowledge, understanding of the person and work of the Holy Spirit. It is critical to your spiritual walk and wellbeing. Jesus said, *"It is expedient that I go away. For if I go not away the Comforter will not come, but if I depart, I will send Him."* Expedient is translated in the following manner.

>NAS/NJKV - advantage

>NIV- good profitable

Jesus wanted the disciples to understand it was to their "advantage," for their "good"; it would be "profitable" for them that He go away so He could send the Holy Spirit to them.

Who Is the Holy Spirit?

Objective:

Help the people discover the person of the Holy Spirit; who He is; what is His personality; and what are His character qualities.

Introduction:

The Apostle Paul declared to the church at Corinth, *"I do not want you to be ignorant (unlearned) about spiritual gifts."* God does not want us ignorant about the things of the Spirit; that is, the person of the Holy Spirit and His working. In the last lesson we established the biblical promise of the Holy Spirit filling the life of the believer.

- First, the prophet Joel - Joel 2:28
- Then, John the Baptist - Matthew 3:11
- Then, Jesus - John 14:15-17
- Then, the Apostle Peter - Acts 2:1-39

Mankind is now living in the time of the Holy Spirit and His work in the lives of all people. The apostolic church experienced the fullness of the Holy Spirit and taught the believers to seek the Holy Spirit and His working in the church.

- Philip went to the community of Samaria (Acts 8:14-17).
- Paul met the disciples at Ephesus (Acts 19:1-7).
- Peter ministered at the house of Cornelius (Acts 10:1-44).

God wants you to have full and correct knowledge of the Holy Spirit, so you can understand His person and His work.

1. We need to ask, "Who is the Holy Spirit?"
    a. He is God
        1. Genesis 1:2 - Referred to as the "Spirit of God"
        2. John 1:32 - His origin and presence is from Heaven
        3. Acts 5:3-4 - Peter refers to Him as God
        4. Matthew 28:19 - Referenced as part of the Trinity of God
        5. First and foremost the Holy Spirit is God.

    b. He is the Executive Agent of the Trinity
        1. Father is the head, Jesus the Son is the Redeemer of mankind, Holy Spirit is the Executive Agent
        2. Define: **Executive:** To complete, follow through to the end, fulfill in accordance with the design **Agent:** act in place of another by his authority
        3. John 15:26
        4. John 16:12-15
        5. Ephesians 1:11-14 - He executes the covenant of God with man and He is the seal of the covenant
        6. Acts 1:8 - He empowers the church to carry the gospel to the world.

2. We need to ask, "What is the Holy Spirit like?"
    a. He is a person
        1. He is referred to as the "Third Person of the Trinity"
        2. "Third" does signify rank or position only in name identifying that He also is deity
        3. He is not just a force or an influence - He has personality and He is a person.

  4. John 14:17, 16:13, 1 John 5:7 - referred to as a person

  5. Acts 5:1-10 - He can be lied to

  6. Ephesians 4:30 - He can feel emotion and be grieved

 b. He is Spirit

  1. Define Spirit: Hebrew (ruah)-wind, breath; Greek (pneuma) wind, breath, air

  2. Genesis 2:7 - God breathed into man the *ruah* of life

  3. John 3:8 - He is the wind that blows

  4. John 4:24 - God is pneuma and man is to worship God in pneuma and truth

 c. He is holy

  1. Sacred - to be spotless, to be above and transcend the creation, majestic, divine

  2. Sanctified - set apart to God for His exclusive use and not for common use to be without defilement or desecration of the unclean

  3. Holy is having no defilement, no flaws, no moral compromise or failure, to be perfect

  4. This is the very nature of the Holy Spirit - He is the very mark and definition of what it means to be without sin, to be pure, clean, undefiled, unsoiled.

 d. The Heavenly Guest

  1. He is the heavenly guest- the old English used the term

"Ghost"(Anglo-Saxon)

2. John 14:17 - with you and shall be IN YOU

3. 1 Corinthians 3:16-17 - local church is the temple of Holy Spirit

4. 1 Corinthians 6:19-20 - our bodies are the temple of the Holy Spirit

5. Romans 8:9 - you must have the Holy Spirit **living** in you to be born again

5. Acts 1:4-5 - God wants us to seek the baptism of the Holy Spirit not just His indwelling of our lives

6. Our lives living in Him.

What is the Work of the Holy Spirit?

Objective:

Help the people discover the person of the Holy Spirit; what are His responsibilities and duties.

Introduction:

We have established the truth of the Holy Spirit being promised to the believer, even to this generation. Look with me at Acts 2:38. 'This promise is to . . .

> You . . .
> To your children . . .
> To all who are afar off . . .
> Even as many as the Lord our God shall call . . .

This promise is inclusive. All who believe in Jesus Christ and receive salvation may receive the promise of the Holy Spirit baptism.

This promise is extensive. It is for every generation of the church, and for every person the Lord calls to salvation.

We have also established the Holy Spirit is deity. He serves as the Executive Agent of the godhead and He is a person, not merely a force. We have looked at His character qualities and what His nature is like.

We must now ask, "What is the work of the Holy Spirit, as the Executive Agent of the godhead?"

1. He is the giver of revelation.
    a. He is to open the eyes of the believers understanding.
        Ephesians 1:15-23
        1 Corinthians 2:9-10
        1 Corinthians 2:14-16

    b. He is to guide the believer into all truth.
        John 14:16-18; 26
        John 16:13-16

2. He is the One who convicts of sin.
    a. He reproves the individual of sin and darkness
        John 16:7-11

    b. He convinces the person that Jesus is Savior.
        John 15:26-27
        1 Cor. 12:1-3
        Eph. 1:15-23

    c. He is the one who draws a person to Jesus Christ.
        John 6:44

    d. He is the one who imparts faith to the heart of the believer.
        Romans 12:3

3. Holy Spirit affects conversion or regeneration of life.
   a. Mankind's need for conversion
      1. Man is separated from God because of sin – Isaiah 59:2
      2. Every person is a sinner from birth – Psalm 51:4-5; Romans 3:10; 3:23; 6:6
      3. Jesus said a person must be converted or born again to have eternal life – John 3:1-3; Matthew 18:3
      4. This denotes a dramatic sudden change in a person's life.

   b. He makes you a new creation.
      Matthew 18:3
      2 Corinthians 5:17-19

   c. He regenerates the inner person.
      Titus 3:5-6
      2 Peter 1:4
      Romans 8:11

   d. He confirms a person has truly been born again.
      1 John 4:13
      1 John 3:24
      1 Corinthians 12:13

   e. He witnesses to the heart of the person they are a child of the living God.
      Romans 8:14-15
      Galatians 4:6

    f. There is no true salvation and conversion without the work of the Holy Spirit.

        Romans 8:9

4. The Holy Spirit is the believer's source of power.

    a. Jesus commanded His disciples to wait for this power.

        Luke 24:44-48

        Acts 1:3-4

        Acts 1:8

    b. The Holy Spirit imparts the manifestation gifts to believers.

        1 Corinthians 12:7-11

How Does a Person Receive the Holy Spirit into Their Life?

Objective:

Help discover the Holy Spirit; how can a person receive the Holy Spirit and His work into their life?

Introduction:

We have established the Holy Spirit is deity; the Executive Agent of the godhead. He is a person, not merely a force. We have looked at His character and nature. We have discovered the work of the Holy Spirit, as the Executive Agent of the godhead.

- He is the agent of truth.
- He is the messenger of conviction.
- He is the One who draws a person to Jesus Christ.
- He is the source of revelation and regeneration.
- He is the source of power in the believer's life.

Now we must ask, how does one receive the Holy Spirit into their life?

1. God created the human body to be the temple of the Holy Spirit.
    a. The local church is the temple of the Holy Spirit.
        1. 1 Corinthians 3:16-17

2. The context is the local church at Corinth.

   3. The believers of the local church are the temple of God, individually.

   4. He is also saying the church gathered together in worship, study, ministry or fellowship is the temple of the Holy Spirit.

 b. God gave a body to human beings to be the temple of the Holy Spirit.

   1. 2 Corinthians 6:11-20

   2. God made the human body for the Lord.

   3. He created the body to be the temple of the Holy Spirit.

   4. God places the Holy Spirit within us.

 c. The Holy Spirit takes up dwelling in a person's body when they receive salvation.

   1. Romans 8:9

   2. The person cannot be saved unless the Holy Spirit comes and lives in them.

   3. When Holy Spirit takes up dwelling they are regenerated and adopted by God.

   4. The Holy Spirit also baptizes the person into the church, the Body of Christ when He takes up dwelling 1 Corinthians 12:12-13.

2. Jesus Christ baptizes believers in the Holy Spirit.

 a. There is a separate work of grace after salvation.

   1. John the Baptist said Jesus would baptize people in the Holy Spirit Matthew 3:11.

   2. Jesus told His followers to wait in Jerusalem for the

baptism of the Holy Spirit Luke 24:44-48; Acts 1:3-4.

3. Jesus' disciples were already saved for their names were written in the book of life Luke 10:20.

4. John the Baptist and Jesus were speaking of a work of the Holy Spirit other than His dwelling in a believer's body.

b. The believers at Samaria received two separate works of the Holy Spirit.

    1. Acts 8:5-17

    2. Philip went to Samaria and preached the Gospel and people were saved and were baptized in water.

    3. When the Apostles in Jerusalem heard about the work they sent Peter and John to Samaria, why?

    4. Specifically for them to pray for the believers, who had been saved, to receive the Holy Spirit.

    5. Holy Spirit had not yet "fallen upon them."

    6. Holy Spirit had taken up dwelling in them but had not baptized them.

c. An interesting event happened for the Gentile believers.

    1. Acts 10:1-44

    2. Peter preached the gospel to the Gentiles for the first time.

    3. The people heard and they believed unto salvation.

    4. They were baptized in the Holy Spirit and saved at the same time.

d. What is baptism?

    1. The Greek word for baptism is *baptizo* (Strong's # 907)

Vine's definition: "To baptize," primarily a frequentative form of bapto, "to dip," was used among the Greeks to signify the dyeing of a garment, or the drawing of water by dipping a vessel into another, etc. Plutarchus uses it of the drawing of wine by dipping the cup into the bowl (Alexis, 67) and Plato, metaphorically, of being overwhelmed with questions (Euthydemus, 277D)[1]

2. The word also was used to describe a sword be tempered to hardness by baptizing it into oil, after it had been heated in fire.

3. Moses' baptism was in the cloud and in the sea Exodus 14:19-21; 1 Corinthians 10:1, 2

4. John the Baptist baptized in water unto repentance Matthew 3:6, John 3:31-33

5. Jesus' disciples baptized in water John 3:22

6. The church is to baptize in water Matthew 28:19; Acts 2:38-41

7. The believer is baptized by the Holy Spirit into the body of Christ Romans 6:3; 1 Corinthians 12:13

8. The believer is baptized into suffering Luke 12:50

9. When someone is baptized in water the person's body is placed into the water, the water is not pour *inside* of them.

10. Baptism in the Holy Spirit is a person's whole being immersed into the Holy Spirit, not the Holy Spirit coming inside of them.

---

[1] Vine's Expository Dictionary of Biblical Words, Copyright (c)1985, Thomas Nelson Publishers)

e. What is the conclusion?

    1. Salvation and the baptism of the Holy Spirit are two separate experiences.

    2. They may happen simultaneously, as in Acts 10:40-44.

    3. They may happen on separate occasions, as in Acts 8:5-17.

    4. The Holy Spirit takes up dwelling *in* a person's body at salvation. Romans 8:9

    5. The baptism of the Holy Spirit is when a person is immersed *into* the Holy Spirit and becomes clothed with power from the Holy Spirit Luke 24:49; Acts 1:3-4, 8

    6. God wants His children to receive both salvation and the baptism of the Holy Spirit in their life.

f. The two experiences have separate and distinct purposes and evidences in the individual's life.

    1. Salvation and the in dwelling of the Holy Spirit will bring forgiveness and deliverance from sin; adopts the person into the family of God; and establishes the person's body as the temple of the Holy Spirit.

    2. Evidence of salvation is new life and the fruit of the Holy Spirit in the person.

    3. The baptism of the Holy Spirit is the immersion of the person into the Holy Spirit for power and supernatural ministry gifts.

    4. The evidence of the baptism of the Holy Spirit is speaking in other tongues. *(This will be an entire study of its own.)*

3. How does someone receive the baptism of the Holy Spirit?

    a. A person must be willing to obey the Lord in all things. Acts 5:32

        1. The Holy Spirit is holy, and the believer must be willing to live in obedience to God and separated unto holiness.

        2. It begins with salvation - Acts 2:38

        3. The believer must set themselves apart unto God exclusively John 14:16-17

        4. This is the foundation for receiving from the Lord.

    b. A person must desire the baptism of the Holy Spirit - John 7:37-39

        1. God will give nothing to a person, unless they want it in their life.

        2. As a natural man desires food and water for the physical body, we must also desire spiritual nourishment - Matthew 5:6

        3. Like a thirsty man in the desert, Jesus said we should thirst for Holy Spirit.

        4. There must be a strong passion for the Holy Spirit fullness.

    c. A person must seek God for the baptism of the Holy Spirit.

        1. Jesus gives to us a three-fold assurance in Luke 11:9-13

        2. If we **ask** we will receive.

        3. If we **seek** we will find.

        4. If we **knock** it will be opened to us.

        5. He was talking about the Holy Spirit, that it would be given to us if we ask.

6. Many fear seeking the Holy Spirit and what will happen to them. Jesus assured we do not need to fear what we will receive when we ask. God will not give to us a serpent, rock or a scorpion- something evil. He is a loving Father who wants to give us good things.

d. A person must wait for the baptism of the Holy Spirit in active praise and worship.
    1. Jesus told them to wait in Jerusalem until they received Holy Spirit baptism from Father - Acts 1:3-4
    2. The waiting was not merely being idle. They were continually in worship and prayer - Luke 24:49-53
    3. Acts 2:1-4

e. A person must yield to the manifestation of the Holy Spirit as He comes upon them.
    1. Acts 2:1-4 – Wind, fire, speaking in tongues came as the people of Jerusalem marveled and thought they were drunk at 9:00 in the morning.
    2. Acts 8:18-19 – there was a manifestation of such power that Simon wanted to buy it for his personal glory.
    3. Acts 10:44-48 – Gentiles spoke in tongues to the amazement of the Jews and they could not deny it was God and the work of the Holy Spirit.
    4. Acts 19:1-7 – Followers of John the Baptist were baptized in the Holy Spirit and began manifesting prophecy and speaking in tongues.

5. Every scripture reveals that the Holy Spirit manifests Himself when He comes upon someone. It may be gentle and quiet, or it may be strong and loud.

6. We must be willing to yield to His working when He comes.

What is the Evidence of the Baptism of the Holy Spirit?

Objective:

Help the people understand what is the evidence of the baptism of the Holy Spirit and what is the purpose of the evidence of the Holy Spirit baptism.

1. The significance of speaking in tongues in your life
    a. The spiritual language is significant because it is a gift from God
       Acts 2:37-39 / 1 Corinthians 12:7-11 / 1 Corinthians 14:1-5

    b. The spiritual language is significant because it enables your prayer life and your personal worship
       Romans 8:26-27 / 1 Corinthians 14:15 / Ephesians 6:18-19

    c. The spiritual language is significant because it strengthens your spiritual life. The gift of tongues and interpretation strengthens the church when it is used in a public meeting.
       1 Corinthians 14:2-4, 5-13 *(note verses 3 and 12)* / Jude 20-21

2. Dispelling some myths about the use of speaking in tongues
    a. It went out of practice with the apostles
       1 Corinthians 14:5 - *"I wish you all spoke with tongues"*
       1 Corinthians 14:18 - *"I thank God I speak in tongues more than you all."* So, they did use the spiritual language

1 Corinthians 14:39 - *"Desire earnestly to prophesy and do not forbid to speak with tongues."* Almost all groups accept this verse and the need for prophecy, but many stop short and do forbid speaking in tongues

Acts 2:38-39 - *"To all who are afar off"*

1 Corinthians 13:8 - *"Whether there be prophesy they shall fall... tongues cease... Knowledge vanish away"* If preaching is still relevant, then, so is the spiritual language

b. Speaking in tongues is of the devil

Matthew 12:22-32 - Jesus warned about religious leaders attributing things to the work of the devil, when it was extending the Kingdom of God. He also warned of the dangers of blaspheming of the Holy Spirit. Pentecostals are advancing the Kingdom of God - how could Satan use that to advance His cause if it is advancing the Kingdom of God?

1 Corinthians 12:1-7 - *"No one speaking by the Spirit of God calls Jesus accursed..."*

c. You require people to speak in tongues to be saved

Romans 8:1-11 – Holy Spirit dwells within for salvation

Acts 8:14-17 – They were saved but did not have the Spirit baptism

Acts 10:44-48 – Gentiles received salvation and Holy Spirit baptism at some time

Acts 19:1-7 – The followers of John the Baptist had to receive true salvation then they received the baptism of Holy Spirit. We do not teach the doctrine you must have speak in tongues to go to heaven

d. The spiritual language is only for private use and should be exercised in a public meeting, the Apostle Paul said so.

> **1 Corinthians 14:13, 22, 26-28, 39** – Paul gave instruction on how *it should be* used in public services
>
> **There are actually three uses for tongues**
>> Private prayer and worship
>> Public prayer and worship
>> Message of edification, exhortation and worship

E. You place more importance upon this than upon the fruit of the Spirit

> **John 15:1-10** – Bear much fruit
>
> **1 Corinthians 13:1-13** – The most important is love
>
> **1 Corinthians 14:1** – You make love your pursuit and spiritual gifts your earnest desire
>
> *Don't get them mixed up*

What is the conclusion then?

God has given you a wonderful gift that will strengthen your spiritual life and take your daily walk with God to a new dimension. He wants you to have it and experience it daily and you need it daily. The Word even instructs you to desire it earnestly. That is what you should be doing.

The Work of the Holy Spirit in Sanctification

Objective:

Help the student understand the biblical model of sanctification and the Holy Spirit's work in administrating that work of grace in the believer's life.

Introduction:

>Luke 1:75 - Serve the Lord *"in holiness and righteousness. . . ."*
>Matthew 5:44 – *"Be ye holy for I am holy."*
>1 Peter 1:22 - *"Purified your soul in obeying the truth. . . ."*
>Hebrews 12:14 – *"Without holiness no man shall see the Lord."*
>1 Thessalonians 4:7 – *"This is your sanctification..."*

The questions to be asked are, "What is sanctification and how is sanctification accomplished in a believer's life?"

1. What is the significance of sanctification?
    a. The meaning of sanctification
        1. The Greek word *hagiasmos* is translated sanctification (Strong's # 38)
        2. Vines defines the word as: . . . *"sanctification," is used of (a) separation to God, 1 Corinthians 1:30; 2 Thessalonians 2:13; 1 Peter 1:2; (b) the course of life befitting those so separated, 1*

Thessalonians 4:3,4, 7; Romans 6:19,22; 1 Timothy 2:15; Hebrews 12:14.

"Sanctification is that relationship with God into which men enter by faith in Christ, Acts 26:18; 1 Corinthians 6:11, and to which their sole title is the death of Christ, Ephesians 5:25,26; Colossians 1:22; Hebrews 10:10,29; Hebrews 13:12. "Sanctification is also used in New Testament of the separation of the believer from evil things and ways. This sanctification is God's will for the believer, 1 Thessalonians 4:3, and His purpose in calling him by the gospel, verse 7; it must be learned from God, verse 4, as He teaches it by His Word, John 17:17,19, cf. Psalm 17:4; 119:9, and it must be pursued by the believer, earnestly and undeviatingly, 1 Timothy 2:15; Hebrews 12:14. For the holy character, hagiosune, 1 Thess. 3:13, is not vicarious, i. e., it cannot be transferred or imputed, it is an individual possession, built up, little by little, as the result of obedience to the Word of God, and of following the example of Christ, Matthew 11:29; John 13:15; Ephesians 4:20; Philippians 2:5, in the power of the Holy Spirit, Romans 8:13; Ephesians 3:16. "The Holy Spirit is the Agent in sanctification, Roans 15:16; 2 Thessalonians 2:13; 1 Peter 1:2; cf. 1 Corinthians 6:11. . . .[2]

3. Robertson gives the following:

> *"Paul includes sanctification in his conception of the God-kind, Romans 1:17 of righteousness (both justification, Romans 1:18--5:21 and sanctification, Romans 6--8). It is a life process of consecration, not an instantaneous act. Paul shows that we ought to be sanctified Romans 6:1--7:6 and*

---

[2] Ibid.

illustrates the obligation by death Romans 6:1-14, by slavery Romans 6:15-23, and by marriage Romans 7:1-6.[3]"

4. Sanctification is setting something apart to God, as holy, for His exclusive use; no longer to be defiled or used as common or unholy.

b. A working definition of sanctification

1. Sanctification is the work of setting one's life apart exclusively for holy use. ie. the holy instruments of the temple; the Ark of Covenant; Aaron and his sons for priesthood.
2. Sanctification involves separation *from* the common and the unclean so the person or the article is not defiled or corrupted.
3. Sanctification also involves a separation *unto* the sacred and the pure, so the item is holy and not unclean.
4. The whole concept of sanctification is, the item or the person has been removed from the common and set apart exclusively for God and to be used in the work and the purposes of the Kingdom of God. Therefore, they are holy as God, Himself, is holy and must not be used to do things that would defile, but are daily growing to become more and more like Jesus Christ in character, attitude and behavior.

c. Sanctification is based upon the believer's position in Jesus.

---

[3] Robertson's Word Pictures in the New Testament, Electronic Database. Copyright (c) 1997 by Biblesoft & Robertson's Word Pictures in the New Testament. Copyright (c) 1985 by Broadman Press

1. Romans 8:1 - There is no condemnation against the believer. Why is this so?
2. Romans 5:1-10 - The believer is justified by the blood of Jesus Christ and have taken on the righteousness of Jesus Christ, Romans 8:4, 2 Corinthians 5:21.
3. Justification is the divine fiat by which God has declared the believer to be judicially just as if they had never sinned.
4. The divine fiat also declares the believer to be the righteousness of Jesus, so they are holy just as He is holy.
5. This is the position of everyone who has been saved by faith, judicially.
6. However, the believer's behavior does not match their position in Christ.

d. The believer's daily life must be transformed.
1. The daily behavior of the believer must be brought into conformity to the judicial declaration of justification.
2. *"For this is the will of God, even your sanctification, that ye abstain from..."* 1 Thessalonians 4:3
3. Romans 12:1 - The believer must be transformed so they are daily living out the *"good, acceptable and perfect will of God."*
4. Transforming the attitude, actions and behavior patterns into holy living is called sanctification.

2. How is the work of sanctification accomplished in the believer's life?
a. Sanctification is not a list of rules.
1. Many believers try to accomplish this task by keeping a list of rules or by practicing religious activity.

2. That is like going back under the Law of Moses and keeping all the Jewish laws and actions.

3. Galatians 3:1-11; 5:22-25

4. The work of sanctification is only accomplished by the power of the Holy Spirit renewing the mind, washing in the blood of Jesus and fruit of Spirit.

b. How does someone put on the new man? Ephesians 4:17-25

1. In Jesus Christ we are new creations, new creatures. Our actions need to reflect who we are positionally *"in Christ."* 2 Corinthians 5:17-21

2. Paul said we are to "put off the old man" and to "put on the new man" listen to these words, "in righteousness and true holiness." How is that done?

3. By the work of the Holy Spirit renewing our mind.

4. The Holy Spirit will take the Word of God and transform the thought patterns, values system, reasoning, ideology, philosophy and memories of the conscious and subconscious mind of the believer (Romans 12:1-2).

5. This enables him to live out the good, acceptable and perfect will of God.

c. How can someone be set free from the slavery of the old desires and habits? Romans 8:11-14

1. The same Holy Spirit that raised Jesus from the dead dwells in the believer.

2. The Holy Spirit imparts His power that gives resurrection life to the human body, so they can live in "newness of life" (Romans 6:3-4).

3. Holy Spirit empowers them to identify their old man is crucified with Christ and is no longer alive (Romans 6:5-7).

4. Holy Spirit empowers them to identify that they are risen to new life in Christ and the members of their body can be used for righteousness not sinfulness (Romans 6:11-14).

5. The power of the Holy Spirit enables the believer to live in freedom, so they do not have to give into the old cravings and desires that once controlled their lives (Romans 8:11-12).

4. Living by the power of the Holy Spirit enables one to live free from slavery to the old habits of the old man (Romans 8:13-16)

d. The Holy spirit brings the fruit of the Spirit.

1. Every believer has the Holy Spirit living within them Romans 8:9

2. Holy Spirit within our life imparts the new nature and divine life source from which every believer may life as a new creature 2 Peter 1:4.

3. Holy Spirit within seeks to bring forth the fruit of the divine life source that lives within the heart of the believer, Galatians 5:22-23.

4. 2 Peter 1:5-8 describes the process that makes that happen.

The Fruit of the Spirit – a More Perfect Way

Objectives:

Instruct the students in the importance of developing God-kind-of-love as the foundation for seeking ministry and the gifts of the Holy Spirit.

Introduction:

Teachings and writings about the baptism of the Holy Spirit seem to focus upon the gifts of the Holy Spirit and person ministry. It is true, Jesus commanded the disciples to wait in Jerusalem and not begin public ministry until they had received the baptism of the Holy Spirit. *"But ye shall receive power, after that the Holy Ghost has come upon you. . .."* Jesus promised.

Previous to this command, Jesus had commanded the disciples to love one another as He loved them (John 13:34-36). The apostle Paul repeated this pattern of teaching in his first letter to the church at Corinth.

> *And God hath set some in the church, first apostles, secondarily prophets, thirdly teachers, after that miracles, then gifts of healings, helps, governments, diversities of tongues. Are all apostles? are all prophets? are all teachers? are all workers of miracles? Have all the gifts of healing? do all speak with tongues? do all interpret? But covet earnestly the best gifts: and yet shew I unto you a more excellent way.*[4]

The "more excellent way" is described by the apostle Paul in the thirteenth chapter of 1 Corinthians as the church loving one other in the same way Jesus Christ loves mankind. The apostle encouraged the church to make love the pursuit of their life while they earnestly seek the gifts of the Holy Spirit (1 Corinthians 14:1).

1. There are three reasons love is "a more excellent way" and it should be the pursuit of the believer's life.
    a. Love is what gives value to our words. *"Though I speak with the tongues of men and of angels, and have not charity, I am become as sounding brass, or a tinkling cymbal"* (1 Corinthians 13:1 KJV).

    b. Love is what gives value to our spiritual gifts. *"And though I have the gift of prophecy, and understand all mysteries, and all knowledge; and though I have all faith, so that I could remove mountains, and have not charity, I am nothing"* (1 Corinthians 13:2 KJV).

    c. Love is what gives value to our work of ministry. *"And though I bestow all my goods to feed the poor, and though I give my body to be burned, and have not charity, it profiteth me nothing"* (1 Corinthians 13:3 KJV).

2. Love is a natural result of Holy Spirit's presence in our life.
    a. What does this kind of love look like?
        1. Read 1 Corinthians 13:3-8 aloud with the students.
        2. Identify the sixteen characteristics of this kind of love.

    b. What is the Greek word used for love in this chapter?

---

[4] 1 Corinthians 12:28-31 KJV

1. The Greek word is *agapeo* (Strong's # 26)
2. Thayer "brotherly love, affection, good will, love, benevolence. . . love feast"[5]
3. "Agape and agapeo are used in the NT

>(a) to describe the attitude of God toward His Son, John 17:26; the human race, generally, John 3:16; Rom 5:8, and to such as believe on the Lord Jesus Christ particularly John 14:21
>(b) to convey His will to His children concerning their attitude one toward another, John 13:34, and toward all men, 1 Thessalonians 3:12; 1 Corinthians 16:14; 2 Peter 1:7
>(c) to express the essential nature of God, 1 John 4:8.[6]

c. The love defined by the apostle Paul in 1 Corinthians 13 is "god-kind-of-love."

>1. This kind of love does not come from the heart of mankind.
>2. This kind of love cannot be attained by personal pursuit or keeping religious duties or the laws of God.
>3. This kind of love must come from the Holy Spirit – Galatians 5:22
>4. This kind of love should grow in our life as a natural

---

[5] The Online Bible Thayer's Greek Lexicon and Brown Driver & Briggs Hebrew Lexicon, Copyright (c)1993, Woodside Bible Fellowship, Ontario, Canada. Licensed from the Institute for Creation Research

[6] Op.cit. Vine's

result of the Holy Spirit living in our heart and our continual fellowship with Him and yielding to His presence and work within us.

3. There are three manifestations of the "more excellent way."
   a. The person will love God with all their being.
      1. Matthew 22:36-40
      2. Love God with all our heart.
      3. Love God with all our soul.
      4. Love God with all our mind.
      5. Love God with all our strength.
      6. This is the greatest commandment.

   b. The person will love other people.
      1. Love others as we love ourselves.
      2. This is the fulfillment of the new commandment Jesus gave in John 13:34-36.
      3. We cannot serve and minister to others at the level necessary for effective ministry without this love.
      4. The manifestation of the Holy Spirit will not be realized to the fullest extent without this kind of love.

   c. Love for the lost of the world
      1. John 3:16 is the very definition of God's heart.
      2. If we are truly walking with the Holy Spirit and being filled with His love, we will love the world the way God loves the world.
      3. The church, without this kind of love, will be as the priest and Levite in the parable of the Good Samaritan (Luke

10:25-37).

4. The ministry of the church is only relevant when we have this kind of love.

d. This love fulfills the law of God.

    1. Jesus said this kind of love holds within it all of the law and the prophets.

    2. When a person loves with "God-kind-of-love" they will keep all of the Ten Commandments.

    3. Keeping the law and the Word of God is a natural outflow of their life, not because of legalism.

    4. This is the fulfillment of Jesus teaching in John 15:9-14.

The Fruit of the Spirit in the Life of the Believer

Objective:

Instruct the students in the importance of developing Christ-like character in their life as source from which ministry and the gifts of the Holy Spirit will flow.

Introduction:

The work of the Holy Spirit begins in the life of a person long before the baptism of the Holy Spirit. His work begins with conviction of sin, then brings new birth and will continue for as long as the person will permit.

When a person has been born again, it is God's will for them to manifest the character of the Lord Jesus Christ (Romans 8:29-30). That is part of what the Apostle Paul was teaching in 2 Corinthians 5:14-18. When a person is born again they are a new creation. *"old things are passed away and all things become new; and all things are of God. . . ."* They receive a new nature with a new life source (2 Peter 1:4) and there should be development of new character. Born again believers are to be manifesting the image of their Heavenly Father and their Elder Brother, Jesus Christ.

We are not able to manifest that character by merely studying human development or behavior modification. It will not happen because we keep a list of rules or try to obey the Ten Commandments. A person may succeed to some degree by doing these things. That is not spiritual development and it will lead to personal pride and spiritual arrogance.

It is only by the inner working of the Holy Spirit within our life that we can take on the character and the image of Jesus Christ. The Bible calls this work the fruit of the Holy Spirit.

> *This I say then, Walk in the Spirit, and ye shall not fulfill the lust of the flesh. For the flesh lusteth against the Spirit, and the Spirit against the flesh: and these are contrary the one to the other: so that ye cannot do the things that ye would. But if ye be led of the Spirit, ye are not under the law. Now the works of the flesh are manifest, which are these; Adultery, fornication, uncleanness, lasciviousness, Idolatry, witchcraft, hatred, variance, emulations, wrath, strife, seditions, heresies, Envyings, murders, drunkenness, revellings, and such like: of the which I tell you before, as I have also told you in time past, that they which do such things shall not inherit the kingdom of God. But the fruit of the Spirit is love, joy, peace, longsuffering, gentleness, goodness, faith, Meekness, temperance: against such there is no law.*[7]

The fruit of the Spirit is the very essence of Jesus Christ's nature and character. It is the will of our Heavenly Father this fruit to be manifested in our life as well. Jesus said that will only be possible by the flow of his life source within us and by allowing Heavenly Father to prune our life on a regular basis.

---

[77] Galatians 5:16-23 KJV

> *I am the true vine, and my Father is the husbandman. Every branch in me that beareth not fruit he taketh away: and every branch that beareth fruit, he purgeth it, that it may bring forth more fruit. Now ye are clean through the word which I have spoken unto you. Abide in me, and I in you. As the branch cannot bear fruit of itself, except it abide in the vine; no more can ye, except ye abide in me. I am the vine, ye are the branches: He that abideth in me, and I in him, the same bringeth forth much fruit: for without me ye can do nothing. If a man abide not in me, he is cast forth as a branch, and is withered; and men gather them, and cast them into the fire, and they are burned. If ye abide in me, and my words abide in you, ye shall ask what ye will, and it shall be done unto you. Herein is my Father glorified, that ye bear much fruit; so shall ye be my disciples.*[8]

Heavenly Father wants us to bear the fruit of the Spirit bountifully, so we reflect His image in our life and so the world will know we are disciples of Jesus Christ. That can only happen as we are yielded to the presence and the work of the Holy Spirit within our whole being. Holy Spirit wants to empower, motivate, direct and discipline our life so we reflect the nature and character of Jesus Christ in our daily behavior. Holy Spirit wants to:

- ✟ Renew our mind, so we can live the good, acceptable and perfect will of God on a daily basis (Romans 12:2).
- ✟ Transform our emotions, so we can minister his grace into every situation and circumstance (1 Peter 4:8-11; James 1:19-27).
- ◆ Reshape our will so we fulfill the calling and purposes of God (John 5:19, 20, 30; Matthew 16:24-26; Matthew 26:36-42).

---

[8] John 15:1-8 KJV

The fruit of the Spirit is manifested in nine character qualities that may be divided into three categories of work.

1. The Holy Spirit wants to shape Christ-like emotions within us.
    a. Love that will be demonstrated to everyone.
        1. Jesus demonstrated love to everyone who came across His life, even His worst enemies.
        2. Jesus taught us to love our enemies (Matthew 5:43-48).
        3. Jesus manifested this love by going to cross for us when we were his enemies (Romans 5:8-10).
        4. This kind of love will cause us to live out the perfect will of God.
    b. Joy that will be demonstrated in the hardest trials
        1. Jesus endured the cross by keeping His eyes on the joy that would be found beyond the present suffering.
        2. Jesus promised to give us His joy (John 15:11).
        3. We are urged to handle life and all it throws at us in the same way (Hebrews 12:1-3).
        4. Joy is that work of the Holy Spirit that enables us to trust God, see the eternal values in all things and rejoice (1 Thessalonians 5:15-18).

    c. Peace that will guard our hearts and minds in all things
        1. Jesus Christ is the Prince of Peace.
        2. Jesus said He would give to us His peace (John 14:25-27; 16:33).
        3. Jesus peace will be like a garrison around our heart and minds (Philippians .4:4-7).

4. Jesus peace is to be the umpire that controls our life (Colossians 3:15).

2. Holy Spirit wants to shape our relationships to be Christ-like.
    a. Long-suffering
        1. Longsuffering is the Greek word, *makrothumia* (Strong's # 3115). The word means
            a) patience, endurance, constancy, steadfastness, perseverance
            b) patience, forbearance, longsuffering, slowness in avenging wrongs"[9]
        2. Colossians 3:12-14 it is one of the qualities a believer is to clothe himself.
        3. Ephesians 4:1-4 this is a very important character quality for unity in relationships.
        4. Christ is our example of enduring hardships (1 Peter 2:21-24).

    b. Gentleness
        1. *chrestotes* Strong's # 5544
            a) moral goodness, integrity.
            b) benignity, kind
        2. The child of God is to live their life with integrity and moral goodness.
        3. That is a significant part of our sanctification (1 Thessalonians 4:1-4).

---

[9] Op.cit., Thayer's

4. Out of the moral goodness and integrity will flow kindness.

c. Goodness

1. *agathosune* Strong's # 19 uprightness of heart and life, goodness, kindness[10]

2. This quality has escaped mankind because of the sin nature and it damages interpersonal relationship (Able and Cain).

3. We are good in certain areas to certain people, then will be evil to others.

4. Heavenly Father wants our life marked by goodness to all men (Luke 2:14).

3. Holy Spirit wants to shape our attitude to be Christ-like.

a. Faith

1. *pistis* Strong's # 4102, it is a conviction of truth, a body of belief. It is also the quality of being faithful.[11]

2. We are to be people of faith, trusting God in four areas:

a. Trust His nature and character (Hebrews 11:6).

b. Trust His Word that it is true and can be relied upon (2 Timothy 3:16).

c. Trust His salvation in Jesus Christ alone (John 3:16; Ephesians 2:8-9).

d. Trust that He will take all that comes our way and work good in our lives (Romans 8:28).

---

[10] Ibid.

[11] Ibid.

3. We are to be people who can be trusted by others i.e. faithful (1 Corinthians 4:2).

4. The is a critical principle of the kingdom (Luke 16:10-12).

b. Meekness

1. *prautes* Strong's 4240, gentle spirit, calm disposition.[12]

2. Moses was called the meekest man in all the earth.

3. Meekness is strength under control.

4. It is someone who can be trusted to be in control of their emotions and behavior no matter how great the adversity or pressurized the circumstance

c. Temperance

1. *egkrateia* Strong's # 1466 – self-control. Someone who has mastery over their emotions, passions and behavior.[13]

2. The child of God must be motivated by the Holy Spirit and his desires, not the passions of emotion or the appetites of the flesh (Galatians 5:16-18).

3. 1 Corinthians 9:24-27 - We live our life in a disciplined manner, as an athlete who is training for the Olympic Games.

4. We are running the race for eternal values.

---

[12] Ibid.

[13] Ibid.

Manifestation Gifts

1 Corinthians 12:1-11

Objective:

Instruct the students in a balanced perspective of the manifestation gifts of the Holy Spirit, 1 Corinthians 12:1-11

Introduction:

The Holy Spirit has been at work from the very first day of creation bringing order from disorder *"And the Spirit moved upon the face of the waters."* His very name indicates He has always moving and at work and He will never stop. His name is Holy Spirit.

Spirit in the Old Testament - *ruwah* in the New Testament - *pnuma*. Both words mean air, wind or breathe. They are always moving and so is the Holy Spirit. He is always moving you just have to open the window of your heart to experience it.

He always has been moving. In the Old Testament Holy Spirit was not only working at the time of creation He was active at the deliverance of Israel from Egypt. He was a cloud by day and a pillar fire by night. He shielded Israel from the Egyptian army and rolled back the waters of the mighty Red Sea making them a wall of water. He was on the Mt. Sinai with Moses and brought in the quail for food. He was visible above the tabernacle and settled down when Moses came into the tabernacle. The Holy Spirit was working with Samson and the prophets Elijah and Elisha.

The Holy Spirit came down like a dove upon Jesus and performed mighty miracles by His hands. The Holy Spirit came down mightily upon the apostles on the day of Pentecost so much so, the people thought they were drunk. He performed miracle after miracle by their hands. Holy Spirit came down powerfully upon the apostle Paul and performed miracles through him.

The Holy Spirit has continued to work in the history of the church. The early church fathers, Waldensians of France, Wycliffe of England, Savonarola of Florence, Huss of Prague, Luther, Calvin, Wesley, Whitfield, Rogues Corner, Cane Ridge, Finney, Moody, Azusa Street, Tennessee, Jesus People, and the Charismatic Renewal.

We need the Holy Spirit to work today. The apostles promised it so in Acts 2:39 and 1 Corinthians 12:7. How does He work? There are nine manifestation gifts that are available through the Holy Spirit.

1. What are the manifestation gifts of the Holy Spirit?
    a. The word of wisdom
        1. Wisdom should be one of the goals of our life. Proverbs 1:1-7; 1:20-23; 9:10; James 1:5-8. It is the ability to view life and circumstance from God's perspective.
        2. Wisdom is a person Jesus Christ. 1 Corinthians 1:24, 30 Proverbs even speaks of wisdom as if it was an individual, even one who was with God at creation (Proverbs 8). Read Proverbs with the idea of wisdom being the Lord Jesus Christ and the harlot as Satan and you receive a fresh insight

into the power of wisdom.

3. Word of wisdom is a special gift from the Holy Spirit that enables us to see the person's need or circumstance with Divine insight and understanding. It enables us to minister with skill and ability that is from God.

4. This gift is received at a time of need or in the middle of a ministry and comes as an impression, an inner voice, a "knowing," or a picture. It will often be that which keeps from doing something that would not have been good or even destructive.

b. The word of knowledge

1. This is a supernatural knowing of facts and details that you have not known previously and would not have been able to know if Holy Spirit had not told you. This is very different from word of wisdom.

2. Word of knowledge is vital for personal ministry and for effective praying. This enables you to assist a person through the four ways of working with problems:

    a) Evasion - not wanting to deal with the problem

    b) Denial - not wanting to admit a problem exists

    c) Transference - dealing with another problem, even imaginary, rather than dealing with the real issue

    d) Facing the problem truthfully, accepting responsibility and dealing with it by the principles of God's Word.

3. Word of knowledge will give you facts and details that will enable you to direct the person to the root problem and the root cause.

4. Word of knowledge is received in the same way as word of wisdom. It may come by an impression, inner voice, a "knowing," or a picture.

c. Faith

1. Faith is absolutely a gift from God (Romans. 12:3, Ephesians 2:8-10).

2. Faith can be increased by the reading of God's Word (Romans. 10:17) and receiving *rhema* ["word" in Romans 10:17] from the Holy Spirit.

3. The "gift of faith" is not the same a saving faith or the trust and confidence that comes from reading and studying God's Word.

4. The "gift of faith" is a supernatural impartation of faith that enables one to believe God for a miracle or a Divine work at a particular moment.

d. Gifts of healing

1. Notice "gifts" is plural for there are many kinds of healing needed.

2. The healing of the soul (mind, will, emotions) as well as different kinds in the body.

3. Wait on the Lord, praying in the Spirit, for His direction and anointing.

4. Minister with gentleness and love following the principles found in James 5:14.

e. The working of miracles

    1. Miracles are the supernatural working of God either outside of the laws of nature or the laying aside of the laws of nature.

    2. There are many examples of miracles in Scripture and in church history.

    3. Notice "miracles" is also plural for there are physical miracles and there are natural miracles.

    4. Physical miracles - raising the dead, body parts grow back, virgin birth, poison from snakes not effecting a man

    5. Natural miracles - sun standing still or going backwards, iron floating, rivers stop flowing, walking on water

f. Prophesy

    1. This is the only gift mentioned in all three arenas of spiritual gifts.

    2. There are three distinct functions of the gift of prophecy.

    3. The motivational gift of prophecy is the sensitivity to right and wrong and a standard of black and white (more in a later teaching).

    4. The Ephesians 4:11 leadership gift is the office of a prophet, like Elijah or Jeremiah, the watchman who calls the warnings of God and foretells events.

    5. The 1 Corinthians 12 gift is the ministry of the Holy Spirit for edification, exhortation or comfort (1 Corinthians 14:3).

    6. It may be given in a public meeting for all who are gathered or it may be a word for an individual.

7. It is received similar to the word of wisdom and the word of knowledge. In this case it may begin coming as a few words and then become clearer as you speak.

8. A word of prophesy should always be judged (1 Corinthians 14:29). It should be a confirmation that brings comfort, assurance or a reproof.

9. When a personal word is given always follow these two steps.

    a) It should be a confirmation to something God has already spoken.

    b) If it is not a clear confirmation shelve it until it is or if it clearly is out of order disregard it completely and dismiss it.

10. The gift of prophesy should be allowed to function freely in meetings within the scriptural order.

    a) With order and discretion - prophecies are not always to be given at the moment they are received.

    b) Wait for right timing and check with the Elders for clarification and confirmation on the timing. Timing is as important as the word itself.

    c) The right timing in a public meeting would be quiet moments between worship songs, following prayer, before a message, during a message [if the word is a confirmation of what is being taught or preached].

    d) Right timing can also be judged by the nature of the word fitting the spirit and atmosphere of the meeting.

e) There should only be two at the most three public prophecies given in one meeting.
f) The Elders should judge each word as they are given.
g) When a word is given that is out of order or scriptural incorrect the Elders are to publicly handle the situation with grace and discretion.

g. Discernment of spirit

1. This is the ability to distinguish the working of Holy Spirit and the working of demonic spirit and to distinguish kinds of spirits.
2. It functions similar to word of knowledge and should function at all times in our lives.
3. It is for the purpose of disarming the enemy and freeing captives.
4. It can distinguish what is at work in difficult situations, in personal conflicts, in a person under attack or in a life out of control.

h. There are three biblical way for using the gift of speaking in other tongues.

1. The first use is to strengthen your spiritual life through personal prayer and worship - 1 Corinthians 14:1-5, Jude 20-21, Romans 8:26, 27.
2. The second is to strengthen your praise, worship and prayer in a public worship celebration or other meetings - 1 Corinthians 14:15, Acts 2:5-13.

3. The third biblical use of speaking in tongues is to bring a message of edification, exhortation or comfort in a public meeting.

4. When using the gift of speaking in tongues in a public meeting (other than for personal worship and prayer) there must always be an interpretation - 1 Corinthians 14:5-14, 1 Corinthians 12:10.

i. What are the biblical guidelines for the public use of speaking in tongues?

1. The use of speaking tongues in a public meeting should not to be forbidden by the leadership - 1 Corinthians 14:39.

2. The Apostle Paul encouraged using speaking tongues for personal worship and prayer in a public meeting as a means for personal spiritual growth and strength - 1 Corinthians 14:15.

3. If someone speaks in tongues for everyone in the meeting to hear (believes they are giving a message in tongue) they should also pray for God to give them the interpretation of the tongue. 1 Corinthians 14:6-13

4. The public use of speaking in tongues is not to be disruptive or disorderly but in the natural flow and spirit of the meeting. 1 Corinthians 14:40

5. If one gives a message in tongues and there is no interpretation there should be no further use of tongues for interpretation in that meeting.

6. When tongues and interpretation does happen in a meeting there should only be two or at the most three in a single meeting. They should happen in proper order -

tongue followed by interpretation - before the second and the third take place.

2. The church must be open to receiving and encourage the gifts of the Holy Spirit to function

    a. The pastor and elders must be functioning in the gifts and teach the congregation how to move in the gifts.

    b. Encouragement for the flowing of the gifts should be given publicly and often.

    c. Room should be made for the gifts in public ministry.

    d. Gifts must function in harmony with the Holy Spirit and in keeping with the order of 1 Corinthians 14.

The Importance of Holy Spirit in Your Life

Objective:

Instruct the students on the scripture significance of Holy Spirit in their life and the importance of seeking his manifested presence every day.

Introduction:

The Old Testament prophet declared to the leaders of Israel

> *This is the word of the LORD unto Zerubbabel, saying, not by might, nor by power, but by my spirit, saith the LORD of hosts.*[14]

A similar declaration was made by the Apostle Paul to the church at Galatia, when he said, *"If we live in the spirit, let us also walk in the spirit"* (Galatians 5:25 KJV). The concept is found in the meaning of the Greek word for "walk." it is the Greek word *stoicheo* (Strong's # 4748), meaning conduct or deportment. Thayer defines the word as follows:

> 1) to proceed in a row as the march of a soldier, to go in order; metaphorically, to go on prosperously, to turn out well 2) to walk, to direct one's life, to live[15]

---

[14] Zacheriah 4:6 KJV

[15] Op.cit. Thayer's

The concept is simple. If the Holy Spirit has given a person new life, then they should let Holy Spirit direct, discipline, empower and motivate their daily behavior. This was the injunction given by the Apostle Paul to the church at Rome.

> *That the righteousness of the law might be fulfilled in us, who walk not after the flesh, but after the Spirit. For they that are after the flesh do mind the things of the flesh; but they that are after the Spirit the things of the Spirit. For to be carnally minded is death; but to be spiritually minded is life and peace. Because the carnal mind is enmity against God: for it is not subject to the law of God, neither indeed can be. So then they that are in the flesh cannot please God.*[16]

There are three important areas in the life of the believer that Scripture declares must happen in the dynamic of the Holy Spirit.

1. Worship must be "in spirit and in truth."
    a. Jesus encountered a woman at well of Jacob - John 4:1-24
        1. Jesus took the more difficult route north to Galilee for He had a divine appointment with a woman at the well of Jacob.
        2. Jesus explained the woman's need for salvation, "living water."
        3. Jesus shared with this woman a great spiritual truth about worship.
        4. All worship of God is founded upon this principle.

---

[16] Romans 8:4-8

b. There are four spiritual principles Jesus taught.
> 1. Worship is not about location or a building.
> 2. God is looking for worshippers.
> 3. God is a spirit and all worship must be directed, empowered, motivated and disciplined by the Holy Spirit.
> 4. Worship must be founded upon the truth of God's Word.

c. Worship in spirit and in truth embraces the presence of God.
> 1. Worship that is not by the dynamic of the Holy Spirit will be carnal having religious form and liturgy but lacking the manifested presence of God.
> 2. Worship that is not by the dynamic of the Holy Spirit will become filled with spiritual pride and for the approval of men.
> 3. Worship that is not by the dynamic of the Holy Spirit will not bring the life-giving flow of the Spirit of God into the hearts of men.
> 4. Worship that is not by the dynamic of the Holy Spirit will bring religious bondage and spiritual dryness.

d. Worship that is by the Holy Spirit brings life.
> 1. The Holy Spirit gives life and living water to the soul and spirit of man.
> 2. The Holy Spirit knows the mind and will of the Father and can direct worship that pleases Heavenly Father.
> 3. The Holy Spirit can lead the worshipper into the very presence of Father God.
> 4. The Holy Spirit can inspire worship that is based upon

the Word of God and will minister the manifested presence of God.

2. Prayer is always to be in the Holy Spirit.
    a. Prayer in the Spirit is a significant part of the armor of God.
        1. The Apostle urged the believers *to "be strong in the Lord and in power of His might"* (Ephesians 6:10).
        2. He admonished them to clothe themselves with the whole armor of God.
        3. A significant part of the armor for the believer is prayer that is Holy Spirit empowered, directed, disciplined and motivated.
        4. Paul said this is the way prayer is "always" to happen.

    b. Why do believers need to pray in the Holy Spirit?
        1. Romans 8:26-27 explains that we do not know how to pray as we should.
        2. The natural mind of man can greatly hinder a person's ability to pray the prayer of faith that will release answers in every situation.
        3. The Holy Spirit knows the mind and the will of Father.
        4. When we allow Holy Spirit to pray through us, He can pray the will of God in every circumstance and we will receive the answer (John. 5:14-15).

    c. What are the consequences of not praying in the Spirit?
        James 4:1-5; 13-18
        1. It is hard to stay awake and to concentrate without getting bored or distracted.

    2. Prayer becomes dry and lifeless words with little effect and meaning.

    3. Prayer is according to human insight and with personal desires and wishes.

    4. The believer will be powerless and anemic spiritually (Jude 20; 1 Corinthians 14:2-4).

3. Study of God's Word is always to be in the Holy Spirit.
    a. Jesus promised the Holy Spirit would be our guide into all truth - John 16:12-15
        1. Jesus said Holy Spirit would guide us into all truth.
        2. Holy Spirit will only speak what Jesus has taught.
        3. Holy Spirit will not reveal facts or doctrine contrary to Jesus teaching.
        4. Holy Spirit will reveal things to come.

    b. Jesus promised the Holy Spirit would be our teacher John 14:26
        1. Holy Spirit will be our teacher and help us remember all we have learned.
        2. Holy Spirit will reveal heresy (1 John 2:26-27).
        3. Holy Spirit will reveal and open our understanding to the truths and principles of God's Word (Ephesians 1:15-23).
        4. The Apostles taught by the power of the Holy Spirit (Acts 15:22-29).

    c. The Holy Spirit reveals the deep things of God.
        1. The natural man cannot receive the deeper things of God but will stay in the milk of the Word of God (Hebrews 5:12-14).

2. 1 Corinthians 2:9-11 - Holy Spirit reveals the things God has for us in secret.

3. 1 Corinthians 2:13-14 - Holy Spirit helps us to rightly appraise the things of God.

4. 2 Corinthians 3:1-18 - Holy Spirit removes the veil of the natural man so we can behold the glory of God.

d. Holy Spirit gives life to the study and the teaching of God's word - 1 Corinthians 3:1-8.

1. Holy Spirit writes the Word of God upon our hearts.

2. Holy Spirit gives life to the Word of God as we study and teach it.

3. Studying the Word of God without the Holy Spirit will cause it to be mere facts and historical record but not Spirit and life.

4. Studying the Word of God without the Holy Spirit will prevent revelation from enlightening the natural mind of man to the inspiration and truth of God.

5. Studying the Word of God without the Holy Spirit will lead to legalism, spiritual pride and hypocrisy.

6. Studying the Word of God without the Holy Spirit will lead to intellectualism and apostasy.

Three Key Principles for Walking In The Holy Spirit

Objective:

Instruct the students in the three biblical principles that govern the believer's walk in the Spirit.

Introduction:

God has promised and given to His people the anointing of the Holy Spirit, whereby Holy Spirit power abides in His children. The anointing was only available to a select few individuals in the Old Testament. After the day of Pentecost, in Acts chapter two, it is available to all who are born again (Acts 2:336-38).

What is the anointing of the Holy Spirit? It is a divine impartation of the God's power and authority that enables an ordinary person to do an extraordinary task.

In the Old Testament, it was represented by the anointing of oil or the wearing of a mantle. Jesus gave the New Testament fulfillment in John 14:13 when He said, *"He that believes on Me, the work that I do so shall he do also and greater works than these shall he do because I go unto my Father."* Jesus commanded His disciples to wait for that promise of the anointing and divine impartation (Luke 24:48 and Acts 1:3-8). God desires for you to have the anointing in your life, so you can be effective in working for the kingdom.

We know God promised the gift of the anointing, is it possible to hinder the anointing from working in your life? The book of Judges records that very thing happening in the life of Samson. Scripture records Samson being used on many occasions to do miracles when, *"The Spirit of the Lord came upon him"* (Judges 14:6, 19; 15:14). The works of great strength done by Samson were not because of his physical strength and dynamic. They were the mighty working of Holy Spirit power through his life.

Judges 16:20-31 records the end of Samson's life. He was a blind prisoner that ground the grain for his enemies. How did such a thing happen to an anointed man of God? The answer is found in Judges 16:20. Samson had been committing adultery with a woman named Delilah. Several times during these escapades he had escaped the enemies snare by the power of the Holy Spirit. This occasion was different. *"And she said, 'the Philistines are upon you, Samson!' And he awoke from his sleep and said, 'I will go out as at other times and shake myself free.' But he did not know that the Lord had departed from him"* (NAS)

Samson thought he would be able to do just as he had done on all the other occasions. *"He did not know that the Lord had departed."* The anointing was not there. He had hindered the anointing from working and did not know it.

That is a picture of the church when she continues her programs and ministries without knowing the anointing has been removed. That is possible. That is reality in too many churches! The scriptures record three ways the anointing of the Holy Spirit can be hindered in the life of an individual or the ministry of a local congregation. We will look at those scriptures to see how you can avoid hindering the anointing of the Holy Spirit in your life.

1. You must learn to live in the power of an un-grieved spirit.
Ephesians 4:22-32

    a. What does it mean to "grieve" the Holy Spirit?

        1. The Greek word for "grieve" is *"lupeo"* Strong's number 3076

        2. It is derived from the word *"lupa"* which means: "sorrow, pain, grief, annoyance, affliction; use of persons mourning"[17]

        3. *lupeo* means

            1) To make sorrowful

            2) To affect with sadness, to cause grief, to throw into sorrow

            3) to grieve, to offend

            4) to make one uneasy, to cause him to have a pang of conscience "[18]

        Paul is saying it is possible to make the Holy Spirit uneasy in your life; make Him feel sad or offended; to cause Him grief.

        4. There are three ways the Holy Spirit is grieved.

    b. Holy Spirit is "grieved" when we live by the old lifestyle.

        1. Living by the old through patterns that callous the heart (4:17-21)

        2. Living by the old values and behavior patterns (4:22-25)

        3. Using the old speech patterns (4:28-29)

        4. God wants to transform our behavior by renewing the spirit of your mind so you put on the new man created in

---

[17] Op.cit., Thayer's

[18] Ibid.

righteousness and holiness (4:23-24).

c. Holy Spirit is "grieved" when we give the enemy areas of jurisdiction in our life

    1. The enemy can establish strongholds in your life. (2 Corinthians 10:3-5, 2 Timothy 2:24-26)

    2. The enemy can establish strongholds in your mind, will, emotions or the flesh.

    3. The enemy seeks to establish strongholds through insufficient repentance or unwillingness to repent (James 4:4-10, Hebrews 12:14-17, 1 Timothy 1:18-20).

    4. The enemy seeks to establish strongholds through the thought life (2 Corinthians 10:4-5, Colossians 2:8).

    5. The enemy will seek to establish strongholds through occult involvement. Even the most innocent involvement with the demonic such as games, figurines, cartoons, etc., can give areas of jurisdiction. Past involvement with cults, the occult, worship of idols, or having an abortion also gives strongholds. (1 Corinthians 10:1-22, Leviticus 17:7, Deuteronomy 32:17, Psalms 106:37)

    6. The enemy will seek to establish strongholds through family lineage (Exodus 20:5, Exodus 34:7, Deuteronomy 5:9, 3:1-4)). This principle can be seen in the area of righteousness as well (2 Timothy 1:4-5, 3:14-16)

d. The Holy Spirit is grieved when you hold unforgiveness, resentment or bitterness in your heart.

    1. Resolve offenses before the end of the day they occur (Ephesians 4:26-27, Psalms 4:1-8)

2. Read Ephesians 4:31-32 from the Amplified Translation

3. We are to forgive one another in same manner Jesus forgives us. Forgive all, unconditionally and ask the Holy Spirit to help you to forget.

4. Unity opens the path for the anointing to flow (Psalm 133:1-3). We seek to live in unity with our marriage partner, children, family, church, neighbors, and coworkers for unity sake and for the anointing.

2. You must learn to live in the power of the Holy Spirit's fire.
   1 Thessalonians 5:12-22

   a. Holy Spirit is a consuming fire.

      1. Jesus baptizes with the Holy Spirit and fire (Matthew 3:11).

      2. The early church received the baptism of the Holy Spirit with fire (Acts.2:1-4).

      3. Apostle Paul urged Timothy to stir up the fire of the Spirit (2 Timothy 1:6-7)

      4. The Apostle warned the church of Thessolonica of the danger of quenching the fire of the Holy Spirit.

   b. The fire of the Holy Spirit is encouraged in our life by:

      1. A heart that honors and respects leaders;

      2. A heart that lives at peace with people around them

      3. A heart of worship;

      4. A heart of prayer;

      5. A heart of thankfulness

      6. A heart that honors spiritual gifts;

      7. A heart that discerns right and wrong;

8. A heart that turns from evil.

c. Guard your heart that you do not put out the fire of the Holy Spirit by:

    1. Harboring wrong thoughts about leaders and those who offend you;

    2. Maintaining a heart of continual praise and worship, especially in your spiritual language;

    3. Keeping a consistent time of prayer and intercession daily

    4. Honor the moving of the gifts of the Holy Spirit, being careful not to be judgmental or critical because of religious training or philosophies of men, and cultivate a desire for them in your life;

    5. Carefully discerning the spirit of truth and error and right and wrong in the media, literature, teachings and your own heart;

    6. Fear the Lord and turn from evil in all of its forms.

3. You must learn to live in the power of a pure heart

   1 Thessalonians 4:1-8

    a. The believer's daily conduct should "please God."

      1. The Thessalonians had received instruction from the Apostle Paul about their "walk."

      2. Walk in the Greek is peripateo (Strong's # 4043) in means: to walk:

         a) To make one's way, progress; to make due use of opportunities

         b) Hebrew for "to live"

            1) To regulate one's life

    2) To conduct oneself
    3) To pass one's life[19]

  3. The daily conduct of the believer should be pleasing to God, accommodate His wishes and desires for their life.

  4. The believer should be maturing so these qualities are increasing in their life.

 b. The sanctified life of the believer includes moral purity

  1. All believers are to live "sanctified" lives.

  2. Sanctified means to be set apart to God for His exclusive use. The believer's life is not to be used for the same purposes and life style as the unsaved world around them. They are to live holy lives that "please God." (see 1 Thessalonians 4:7)

  3. Moral purity, sexual purity, is a significant part of the sanctified life.

  4. It is a commandment of the Lord Jesus Christ that believers abstain from sexual and moral impurity.

  5. It is significant to note the Apostle Paul is writing to believers about sexual purity and proper conduct in living morally pure.

  6. It is an important issue for the body of Christ today, as well.

 c. The believer must learn how to possess their "vessel" in sanctification and honor

  1. Vessel is a Greek word that may be used for both your

---

[19] Ibid.

own body and also for the wife.

2. The believer is to know how to possess their wife and their own body in sanctification (holiness, God's exclusive use) and honor (respect, reverence)

3. The believer is to live by a different sexual standard than the philosophy, values, fashions, and ideology of the world who does not know Christ.

4. They are not take advantage of or defraud their fellow brother and sister in the Lord.

d. A different standard of behavior is set for the believer.

1. God has called us to live holy lives (v. 7) that are lived by a different value system than the unsaved world around us.

2. The believer must guard against practices that would take advantage or defraud their brother or sister, or themselves.

- Dress that is revealing or sensuous
- Behavior that would be alluring or tempting
- Dating practices that would take advantage of the dating partner sexually
- Inappropriate comments or jokes
- Masturbation
- Movies that have any nudity, cursing, etc.
- Pornographic literature or internet sites

3. This generation has brought the world's standards of sexual conduct into the family of God, saying, "As long as they are married, and both are consenting, nothings is impure in marriage." Paul did not agree. "Possess your *wife* in sanctification and honor," he said.

4. Hebrews 13:4 agrees with the Apostle Paul.

Let marriage be held in honor - esteemed worthy, precious, [that is] of great price and especially dear - in all things. And thus let the marriage bed be (kept undishonored,) undefiled; for God will judge and punish the unchaste (all guilty of sexual vice) and adulterous.[20]

5. The marriage bed can be defiled and dishonored when one or both parties allow "sexual vice" or adultery to be involved in their lives.

6. When the married couple brings the unsaved world's standard of sexual practices (pornographic books and movies, perversion of any kind) into their marriage they are not "possessing their vessel in sanctification and honor." This has become common practice among Christian couples today, as is even sanctioned by some Christian marriage counselors and seminar teachers.

e. This behavior "rejects" the truth of God's Word and the Holy Spirit's influence.

1. The Apostle Paul made it clear. When you practice such behavior you are rejecting God's standard of holiness.
2. The individual also rejects the work of the Holy Spirit in their life.
3. Galatians 5:16-17

---

[20]Hebrews 13:4 Amplified Translation

Selected Bibliography

Cho, Paul Yonggi. *The Fourth Dimension*. Logos: Plainfield. 1979.

Clarno, Eloise. Ed. *A Reader on the Holy Spirit*. International Church of the Foursquare Gospel: Los Angeles. 1993.

Conn, Charles W. *A Balanced Church*. Pathway Press: Cleveland. 1975.

Ervin, Howard M. *Spirit Baptism, A Biblical Investigation*. Hendrickson Publishers: Peabody. 1987.

Gee, Donald. *Concerning Spiritual Gifts*. Gospel Publishing House: Springfield. 1949.

Hayford, Jack W. *The Beauty of Spiritual Language*. Thomas Nelson Publishers: Nashville. 1996.

Robeck, Cecil M., Jr. Ed. *Charismatic Experiences in History*. Hendrickson Publishers: Peabody. 1985.

Sanders, J. Oswald. *The Holy Spirit and His Gifts*. Zondervan Publishing House: Grand Rapids. 1940.

Simpson, A.B. *The Holy Spirit*, 2 Volumes. Christian Publications: Harrisburg. N.D.

Triplett, Bennie S. *A Contemporary Study of the Holy Spirit.* Pathway Press: Cleveland. 1970.

Wigglesworth, Smith. *Ever Increasing Faith.* Gospel Publishing House: Springfield. 1924.

Made in United States
Orlando, FL
09 July 2022

19577611R00049